W9-CTP-571

ouch

FEELINGS

ALIKI

MULBERRY BOOKS · New York

with special thanks to
Jolly, Susan, Patty,
Catherine, Sandy, and Jason

Library of Congress Cataloging in Publication Data   Aliki.   Feelings.
Summary: Pictures, dialogs, poems, and stories portray various emotions we all feel: jealousy, sadness, fear, anger, joy, love, and others. 1. Emotions—Juvenile literature. [1. Emotions] I. Title.
BF561.A47 1984   152.4   84-4098   ISBN 0-688-06518-X

This book is for
Alexa
my model, my Gemini

I thought
you were
never
coming
back.

I HAVE FEELINGS

Your feelings
can be touched
by seeing something.

— really?

THE CROCUS
A DIALOGUE

Girl: A crocus!

Friend: The first sign of spring!

Girl: Listen to the birds.

Friend: Soon we can ride our bikes again.

Girl: I feel all tingly inside.

Friend: You're getting spring fever.

Girl: I think I'll write a poem.

oh
ding-a-ling
spring!

oh
inch-a-long
worm!

feelings can be touched by someone. oh.

YOU ARE INVITED TO MY PARTY

you are invited...

YIPPY

HIPPY YIPPY YOPPY YOOO

I can't wait till Saturday!

I'll make Alfred a present right now.

I'm HAPPY HAPPY HAPPY

WHAT TOM DID

WHAT JOHN DID

The dragon moved closer. It took a deep breath and coughed out a red billow of fire. Smoke filled the boy's eyes. He felt sick. He shut his eyes and rubbed them in pain. Just then he felt something grab at his arm. It was the dragon.

The boy opened his eyes. His blood ran cold. His hair stood on end. He was petrified. Chills ran up and down his spine. He had never felt so afraid. Two balls of fire stared back at him. The dragon's long green claws were grabbing at his neck. The boy was paralysed with fear.

The dragon's gigantic mouth opened. Thousands of teeth shone in the dark. The smell of eaten children filled the boy's nostrils.

"WHAT ARE YOU DOING IN MY CAVE?" bellowed the dragon. But before the frightened boy could answer . . .

ALICIA HAS THE MOST BEAUTIFUL CURLY HAIR OF ALL MY FRIENDS.

CURLY HAIR?

I'd... I'd...

like to CHOKE Alicia.

Elizabeth likes her more than me.

What's wrong with straight hair?

What's wrong with STRINGY hair, if you're nice?

I HATE ALICIA.

GRRRR.

Kate's jealous.

She's green with envy!

she looks red to me.

THE PAPER AIRPLANE

This is your conscience speaking: DON'T DO IT.

gulp

I told you.

DAMIAN, DID YOU THROW THIS?

She caught me.   He feels ashamed.

My face is hot. COME HERE. He feels embarrassed.

I shouldn't have done it.   He feels guilty.

What's going to happen?   He feels afraid.

Is she going to tell? I WARNED YOU. He feels humiliated.

I'LL HAVE TO PUNISH YOU. I'll bet he's sorry.

I'm sorry. REMEMBER THAT NEXT TIME. He will.

Nothing is worth this.   Crime does not pay.

HERE I GO!
I'M GOING TO JUMP
FROM THE HIGHEST DIVING BOARD.
I AM MISTER BOLD,
BRAVE AS MIGHTY MOUSE.

Some
people
aren't
afraid
of
anything.

Show
off.

13

WE HAVE A NEW GIRL IN CLASS

I'd
like
to
hide.
They're
all
staring
at
me.
Is
she
laughing
at
me?

I
wish
I
could

fall
through
the
crack
in
the
floor...

she
looks
shy.

You'd
feel
shy, too,
if you
were
standing
up there.

she
looks
nice.

Hello.
My name
is Patricia.

14

WHISKERS

Whiskers died.

Oh, poor Whiskers.

You had her so long.

I'm sad for you.

She was old.

She was sick.

She had to die sometime.

My heart is broken.

She was silly.

She was funny.

We'll miss you, Whiskers.

"sticks and stones can break your bones but words can never hurt you."

That's what you think.

E MY CRAYONS I KNEW IT WAS YOU YOU ALWAYS
HINGS WITHOUT ASKING HOW DARE YOU DO I TAKE
INGS WITHOUT ASKING I BET YOU BROKE ALL
THE POINTS IF THERE'S ONE THING THAT
GETS ME MAD IT'S SOMEONE TAKING
MY THINGS WITHOUT ASKING
I BET YOU'RE NOT
EVEN SORRY

I just borrowed them.

17

18

HERE, HAVE SOME

feeling quiet

There's nothing to do.
I made my bed.
I practiced my recorder.
I read all my books.
I'm sick of puzzles.
I'm bored,
    bored,
        BORED.

She sounds
lonely to me.

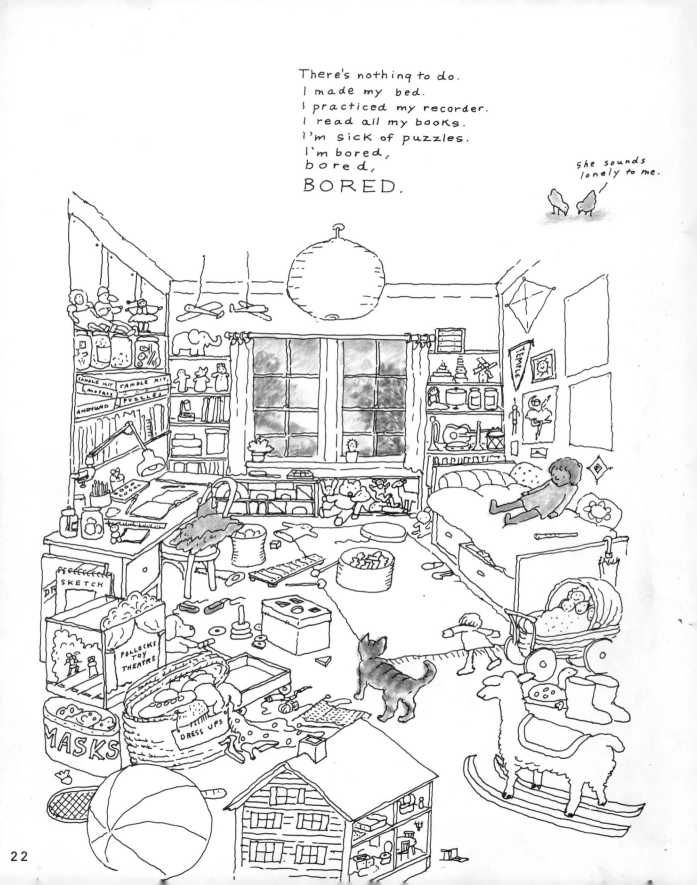

TELEPHONE, ELIZABETH

Hello.

Hi, Kate.

Nothing.

I'm bored.

Can you come over?

YOU CAN?

RIGHT NOW?

I'll meet you.

Kate's my best friend!

I'm going to send her a Valentine.

A happy ending.

Hi, Kate!

Hello, Elizabeth!

LOST
AND
FOUND

24

CHICKEN POX

I don't feel well.

I feel terrible.

I feel horrible.

Tell everybody.

DID YOU MISS ME? I HAD THE CHICKEN POX. THE DOCTOR SAID IT WAS THE WORST CASE HE HAD EVER SEEN. I FELT SICK AND TERRIBLE. I HAD BIG RED SPOTS ALL OVER. I COULD HARDLY BREATHE. MY HEAD WAS SO HOT IT MELTED ALL THE ICE CUBES IN THE TOWEL IN TWO SECONDS. MY FEET WERE FROZEN. I COULDN'T EAT. MY TEMPERATURE WAS SO HIGH IT ALMOST BROKE THE THERMOMETER. I POURED SWEAT. I WAS SO TIRED I COULD HARDLY LIFT A FINGER. I DIDN'T EAT FOR DAYS AND DAYS AND DAYS. MY MOTHER WAS AFRAID I WOULD STARVE. I HAD TO TAKE THIS HORRIBLE MEDICINE THAT MADE ME THROW UP ALL OVER THE PLACE. THE DOCTOR CAME AND GAVE ME A SHOT. IT FELT LIKE A TEN-FOOT NEEDLE. NOTHING HELPED. I NEVER FELT SO MISERABLE.

ONE DAY I SLEPT 15 HOURS. MY POOR FATHER THOUGHT I WAS IN A COMA. I WAS DELIRIOUS. I NEVER THOUGHT I'D GET BETTER. I NEVER THOUGHT I WOULD BE ABLE TO GET UP AGAIN AND WALK AND COME TO SCHOOL. I THOUGHT I WOULD NEVER BE ABLE TO TELL YOU . . .

THE BIRTHDAY

A STORY IN SIX PARTS

and many moods.

moods change like feelings.

PART ONE: MORNING

It's saturday!

It's my birthday!

I'm so excited.

I wonder what presents I'll get.

PART TWO: THE PRESENT

What a great...

sundial.

It's a sundial.

I made it.

I shouldn't have.

I should have bought the screw driver instead.

I feel stupid.

Alfred doesn't even know what it is.

YOU MADE IT?

I like making presents.

It must have taken you a long time.

I thought you bought it!

Anyone can BUY a present.

They like it.

Here's how it works.

oh! ah. ah.

They're all admiring my sundial.

I feel proud of myself.

He should.

PART THREE: PIN THE TAIL

PART FOUR: BIRTHDAY CAKE

PART FIVE: GOODBYE

PART SIX: NIGHT

YOUR ATTENTION, PLEASE

HOW DO YOU FEEL?

Love is the
best feeling.

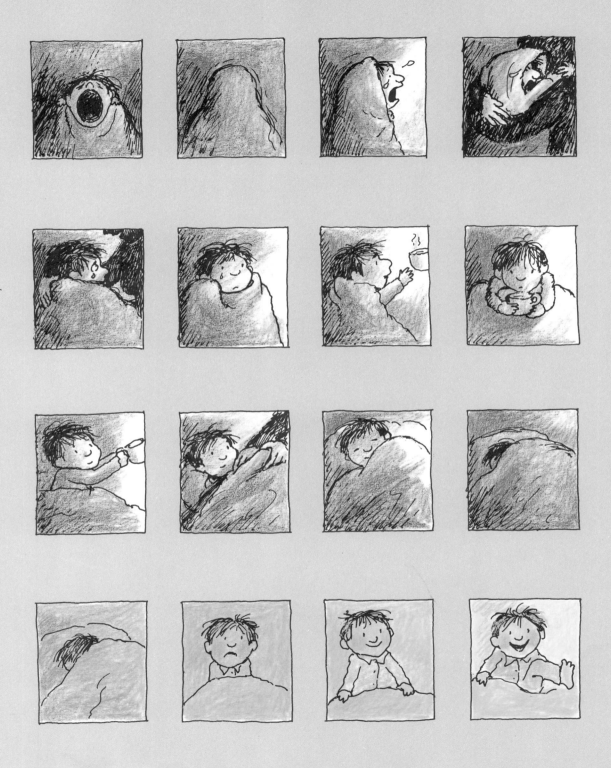